Police Cars

Julie Murray

Abdo Kids

MY COMMUNITY: VEHICLES

abdopublishing.com

Published by Abdo Kids, a division of ABDO, PO Box 398166, Minneapolis, Minnesota 55439.
Copyright © 2016 by Abdo Consulting Group, Inc. International copyrights reserved in all countries.
No part of this book may be reproduced in any form without written permission from the publisher.

Printed in the United States of America, North Mankato, Minnesota.

102015

012016

THIS BOOK CONTAINS
RECYCLED MATERIALS

Photo Credits: iStock, Shutterstock

Production Contributors: Teddy Borth, Jennie Forsberg, Grace Hansen

Design Contributors: Candice Keimig, Dorothy Toth

Library of Congress Control Number: 2015941777
Cataloging-in-Publication Data
Murray, Julie.
 Police cars / Julie Murray.
   p. cm. -- (My community: vehicles)
ISBN 978-1-68080-132-3
Includes index.
1. Police vehicles--Juvenile literature.   I. Title.
629.222--dc23
                          2015941777

Table of Contents

Police Car

Whoo! Whoo!

Cam hears the police car.

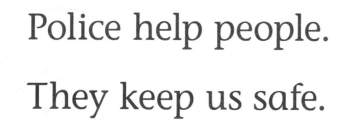

Police help people.

They keep us safe.

Some police cars are blue
and white. They can go fast.

They have loud sirens.

Their lights flash.

The cars have **two-way radios**.
Police officers can talk to
each other.

They have video cameras.

They also have computers.

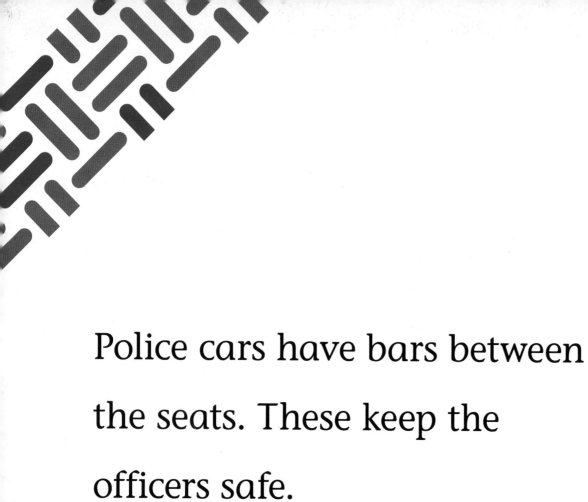

Police cars have bars between the seats. These keep the officers safe.

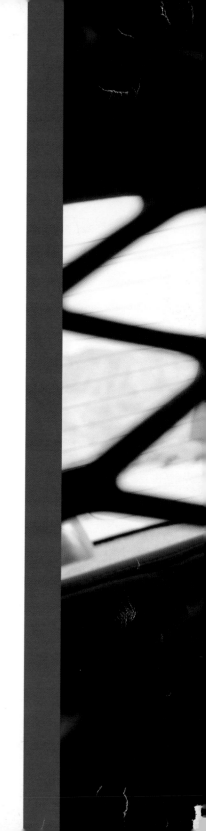

Some police cars are **K-9 units**.

The dogs help the police.

Have you seen a police car?

Parts of a Police Car

bars

lights

computer

two-way radio

Glossary

K-9 unit
police dogs and their handlers
whose job it is to track criminals
and detect substances.

two-way radio
a radio that can give and receive
voice communication.

Index

abdokids.com

Use this code to log on to abdokids.com and access crafts, games, videos, and more!

Abdo Kids Code:
MPK1323